Yellow Umbrella Books are published by Capstone Press
151 Good Counsel Drive, P.O. Box 669, Mankato, Minnesota 56002
http://www.capstone-press.com

1 2 3 4 5 6 07 06 05 04 03 02

Library of Congress Cataloging-in-Publication Data
Franco, Betsy.
    Subtraction fun/by Betsy Franco.
    p. cm. — (Math)
    Includes index.
    Summary: Illustrations and simple text show how to use subtraction to get the answers to everyday questions.
    1. Subtraction—Juvenile literature. [1. Subtraction.] I. Title. II. Series.
QA115 .F73 2002
513.2′12—dc21   2001008009

Editorial Credits
Susan Evento, Managing Editor/Product Development; Elizabeth Jaffe, Senior Editor;
Dawn Harris, Designer; Kimberly Danger and Heidi Schoof, Photo Researchers

Photo Credits
Cover: Bruce Coleman; Title Page: David F. Clobes (upper left), David F. Clobes (upper right), Orion/International Stock (lower left), Jack Glisson/Kentucky Up Close (lower right); Page 2: K.D. Dittlinger (left and right); Page 3: K.D. Dittlinger; Page 4: Jack Glisson/Kentucky Up Close; Page 5: Jack Glisson/Kentucky Up Close; Page 6: David F. Clobes; Page 7: David F. Clobes; Page 8: Orion/International Stock; Page 9: Deneve Feigh Bunde/Unicorn Stock; Page 10: Ken Lax; Page 11: Ken Lax (top and bottom); Page 12: David F. Clobes; Page 13: David F. Clobes; Page 14: David F. Clobes; Page 15: David F. Clobes; Page 16: Sunstar/International Stock (all photos)

SUBTRACTION
FUN

BY BETSY FRANCO

Consulting Editor: Gail Saunders-Smith, Ph.D.
Consultants: Claudine Jellison and Patricia Williams,
Reading Recovery Teachers
Content Consultant: Johanna Kaufman,
Math Learning/Resource Director of the Dalton School

Yellow Umbrella Books

an imprint of Capstone Press
Mankato, Minnesota

Subtraction is taking one number away from another.
Sometimes when we want to figure things out, using subtraction can help.

Let's see what we can find out
when we use subtraction.

You can use subtraction to find out how many more balloons she has than he has.

How many balloons does she have? She has **7** ballons.

How many balloons
does he have?

He has **3** balloons.

You can use a minus sign
to show subtraction.

7 - 3 = 4

She has **4** more balloons
than he has.

You can use subtraction to find out
how much more she will pay
for **1** candy snack
than for **1** bubble gum ball.

The candy snacks cost **10¢** each.

The bubble gum
balls cost **5¢** each.

You can use a minus sign
to show subtraction.

10¢ - 5¢ = 5¢

She will pay **5¢** more
for **1** candy snack.

You can use subtraction to find out how many puppies are left playing on the beach after **1** puppy goes home.

We see **3** puppies playing on the beach.

One puppy goes home to play with his ball.

3 - 1 = 2

Two puppies are left playing on the beach.

You can use subtraction to find out how much taller she is than he is.

She is **5** feet tall.

He is **4** feet tall.

5 - 4 = 1

She is **1** foot
taller than he is.

You can use subtraction to find out how many more flowers he needs to make **7** flowers.

He has **3** flowers.

He wants to have **7** flowers.

7 - 3 = 4

He needed **4** more flowers
to make **7** flowers.

You can use subtraction
to find out how many
of the total number
of hamsters are hiding.

There are **5** hamsters in all,
but you can only see **3** of them.

$$5 - 3 = 2$$

Now you can see all the hamsters.
Two of them were hiding
in the chips.

Using subtraction is a lot of fun!

Kim and Max — Max

= Kim

Words to Know/Index

Word Count: 336
Early-Intervention Level: 14